NORTH AMERICAN
ANIMALS

ARMADILLOS

by Jill Sherman

AMICUS | AMICUS INK

Amicus High Interest and Amicus Ink are imprints of Amicus
P.O. Box 1329, Mankato, MN 56002
www.amicuspublishing.us

Library of Congress Cataloging-in-Publication Data
Names: Sherman, Jill., author.
Title: Armadillos / by Jill Sherman.
Description: Mankato, Minnesota : Amicus/Amicus Ink, [2019] |
Series: North American animals | Audience: K to grade 3. | Includes
bibliographical references and index.
Identifiers: LCCN 2017047791 (print) | LCCN 2017049230 (ebook) | ISBN
9781681514956 (pdf) | ISBN 9781681514130 (library binding) | ISBN
9781681523330 (pbk.)
Subjects: LCSH: Armadillos--Juvenile literature.
Classification: LCC QL737.E23 (ebook) | LCC QL737.E23 S54 2019 (print) |
DDC 599.3/12--dc23
LC record available at https://lccn.loc.gov/2017047791

Photo Credits: Bill Draker/imageBROKER/AgeFotostock cover;
klausbalzano/iStock 2, 20-21; directphoto.bz/Alamy Stock Photo 4–5;
Danita Delimont/Getty 6–7; Michael & Patricia Fogden/Minden Pictures/
SuperStock 8–9; Heidi and Hans–Juergen Koch/Minden 11, 18–19; Arto
Hakola/Getty 12–13; Waddell Images Shutterstock 14–15; Ian & Kate
Bruce/Flickr 16; George Grall/National Geographic/SuperStock 22
Special thanks to conservation photographers Ian & Kate Bruce for use of
their photo. https://www.flickr.com/people/ian-bruce/

Editor: Wendy Dieker
Designer: Aubrey Harper
Photo Researcher: Holly Young

Printed in China

HC 10 9 8 7 6 5 4 3 2 1
PB 10 9 8 7 6 5 4 3 2 1

TABLE OF CONTENTS

ARMORED ANIMAL

Armadillos are tough. They are covered with bands of bony **plates**. These bands fit together. They are like a suit of armor. Armadillos are well protected.

AMERICAN MADE

There are 21 **species** of armadillos. Only two kinds of armadillos live in North America. They are the nine-banded and northern naked-tailed armadillos. All the other kinds live in South America.

BANDED MAMMALS

Armadillos are **mammals**. Look closely to see hairs sticking out under the shell. Like other mammals, they give birth to their young. Mothers feed their babies milk from their bodies.

Check This Out

Armadillos are the only mammals that have shells.

MANY HABITATS

Armadillos love shade. They live in grasslands and forests. Wherever they are, expect sandy soil that is easy to dig in.

Check This Out
Armadillos stand up to sniff the air. Is there an enemy nearby?

DIGGING TO SAFETY

Pumas and bears and alligators! Oh my! These animals hunt armadillos. To stay safe, armadillos quickly **burrow** into the ground. Their armor protects from above. Their soft bellies are safe below.

DIG IN!

Armadillos use long claws to dig for food. They sniff out bugs. With long, sticky tongues, they lick up bugs. Armadillos also eat plants and fruit. They are **omnivores**.

ALL ALONE

Most armadillos live alone. But when weather cools, they get together. Groups sleep in the same burrow at night. Their body heat keeps them warm.

Check This Out
Armadillos are only awake for 6 to 8 hours a day!

ARMADILLO PUPS

Baby armadillos are called pups. One to twelve pups are born at a time. At first, they have soft, gray shells. After a few days, their shells harden.

FAR AND WIDE

Nine-banded armadillos have been on the move. For the past 100 years, they have been spreading north. Some have reached Illinois and Nebraska! Maybe one day, you will spot an armadillo in your neck of the woods.

A LOOK AT ARMADILLOS

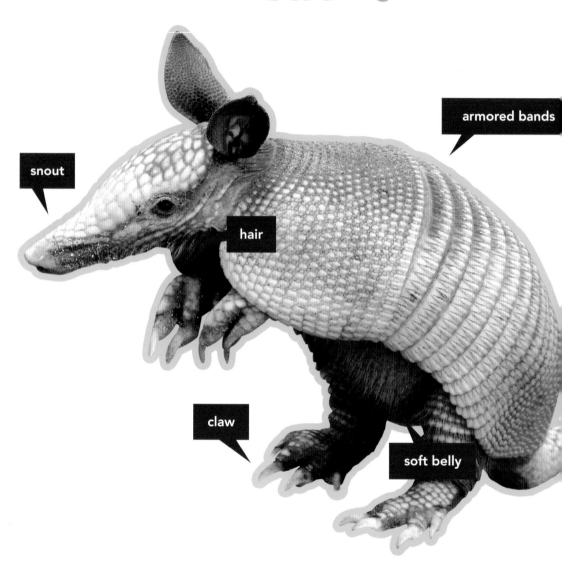

armored bands

snout

hair

claw

soft belly

WORDS TO KNOW

burrow – to dig into the ground.

mammal – a warm-blooded animal with a backbone that has hair, gives live birth, and feeds milk to its young.

omnivore – an animal that eats both plants and animals.

plates – bony sections that make up an animal's shell.

species – a type of animal in a group of animals that are the same and share characteristics.

LEARN MORE

Books

Borgert-Spaniol, Megan. *Nine-banded Armadillos*. Minneapolis: Bellwether Media, 2016.

Davin, Rose. *Armadillos*. North Mankato, Minn.: Capstone Press, 2017.

Websites

National Geographic Kids: Armadillo Alley
http://kids.nationalgeographic.com/kids/games/actiongames/armadilloalley/

San Diego Zoo: "Shell"o, Armadillo!
http://kids.sandiegozoo.org/stories/shello-armadillo

INDEX